# DRAW AMAZING ANIMAL MASH-UPS

BY MARI BOLTE
ART BY ALAN BROWN

CAPSTONE PRESS
a capstone imprint

Edge Books are published by Capstone Press,
1710 Roe Crest Drive, North Mankato, Minnesota 56003
www.mycapstone.com

**Library of Congress Cataloging-in-Publication Data**
Names: Bolte, Mari, author.
Title: Draw amazing animal mash-ups / by Mari Bolte.
Description: North Mankato, Minnesota : Edge Books, Capstone Press,
2018. | Series: Drawing mash-ups | Includes bibliographical references
and index. | Audience: Ages 9-12. | Audience: Grades 4 to 6.
Identifiers: LCCN 2017021449 | ISBN 9781515769361 (library binding) |
    ISBN 9781515769408 (ebook pdf)
Subjects: LCSH: Animals in art--Juvenile literature. | Anthropomorphism
    in art—Juvenile literature. | Drawing—Technique—Juvenile literature.
Classification: LCC NC1764.8.A54 B65 2018 | DDC 743.6—dc23
LC record available at https://lccn.loc.gov/2017021449

**Editorial Credits**
Brann Garvey, designer; Kathy McColley, production specialist

**Image Credits**
Illustrations: Alan Brown; Photos: Capstone Studio: Karon Dubke, 5 (all);
Backgrounds and design elements: Capstone

Printed and bound in the USA.
010364F17

# TABLE OF CONTENTS

# DRAW ON THE WILD SIDE

Do you like to let your imagination run loose? Now you can! Combine two (or more!) unlikely ideas together to create an animal mash-up that defies nature. Use the ideas in the book, and then re-mash them to make something that roars, whinnies, and slithers! Challenge your friends to see who can draw the most out-there art.

# MATERIALS

The artwork in this book was created digitally, but that doesn't mean your own art can't look equally amazing.

It all starts with a pencil and paper! Use light pencil strokes to shape your creation. Shading, hash marks, and curved lines can really make your mash-ups pop off the page.

When you're happy with how your sketches look, darken the pencil lines and erase any overlapping areas. Use a pen to outline and add shadows and detail.

Markers or colored pencils will truly bring your art to life. Experiment with shading, outlines, blending, or using different shades of the same color to make gradients. Or try out a new art supply! Chalk or watercolor pencils, oil crayons, or pastels could add an extra challenge.

# 221B BANANA STREET

This detective is smarter than the average chimp.
He's on the case – to find the missing case of bananas!

STEP 1

STEP 3

STEP 2

## STEP 4

**TIPS**

Put this crime-fighting chimp in all sorts of situations. Have him climbing a fire escape to chase a criminal or driving a car with his feet!

## STEP 5

## FINAL!

# LUCHA-ROAR

Lucha libre fighters, or luchadore, wear a mask in the ring. This bear has its own natural mask! Sometimes wrestlers must remove their mask after losing. Good thing this bear never loses!

STEP 1

STEP 2

STEP 3

STEP 4

STEP 5

## TIPS

Fill the ring with other lucha libre mash-ups! What would a fighting lion look like? Or try something funny or unexpected, like a wrestling penguin or sloth.

FINAL!

# CONSTA-BULL

The consta-bull is here to lay down the law. But don't let his stern face confuse you – he's really just a big puppy dog.

STEP 1

STEP 2

STEP 3

STEP 4

FINAL!

STEP 5

# PURR-FECT DISMOUNT

This cat may have nine lives, but she's hoping to score a 10. It's easy to stick your landing when you've got claws on all four feet!

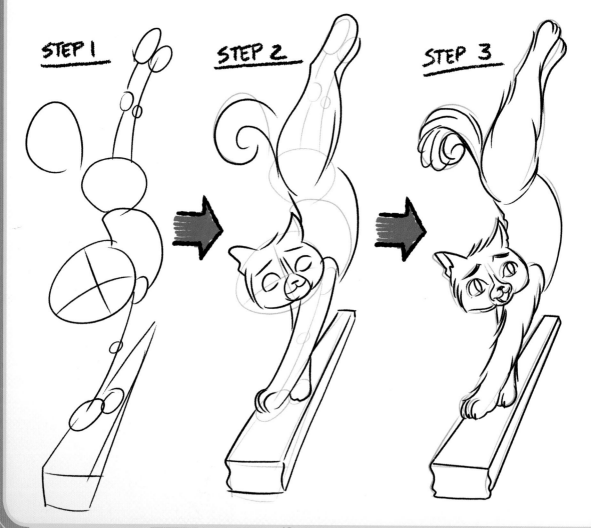

STEP 1

STEP 2

STEP 3

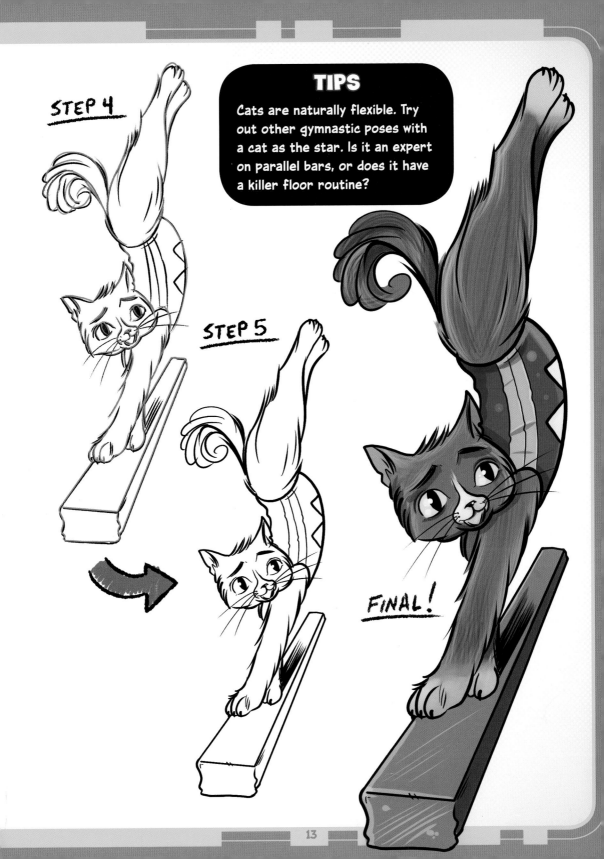

STEP 4

**TIPS**

Cats are naturally flexible. Try out other gymnastic poses with a cat as the star. Is it an expert on parallel bars, or does it have a killer floor routine?

STEP 5

FINAL!

# RAT RACER

Wheels in cages just go 'round and 'round. Escape the wheel and go off-roading. Race other rats, or test your skills by flying over jumps or through muddy bogs.

**STEP 1**

**STEP 2**

**STEP 3**

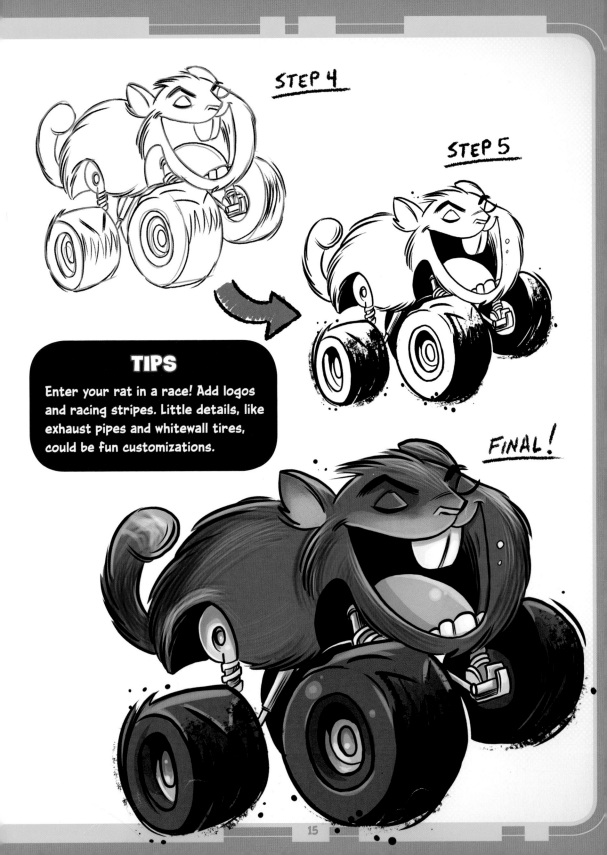

STEP 4

STEP 5

**TIPS**

Enter your rat in a race! Add logos and racing stripes. Little details, like exhaust pipes and whitewall tires, could be fun customizations.

FINAL!

# FIREFIGHT AT THE CIRCUS

Elephants can hold 2.5 gallons (9.5 liters) of water in their trunks. Armed with a water supply, an axe, and an elephant's strength, this firefighter is on the job.

STEP 1

STEP 2

STEP 3

STEP 4

STEP 5

FINAL!

## TIPS

How does this firefighter get from place to place? Does he ride in a fire truck, or use another form of transportation? Balancing on a giant ball won't get him there very fast – but it will look cool!

# BOXEROO

Duck, weave, bob, and bounce! This roo is ready to box his way to the top. Who's ready to take on this champion from down under?

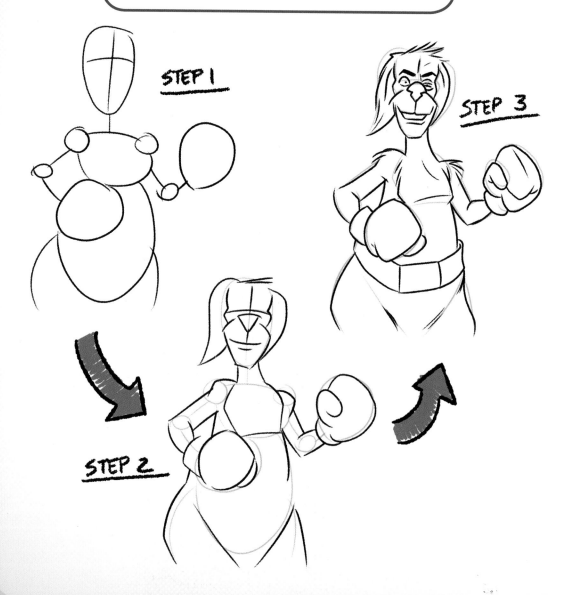

STEP 1

STEP 2

STEP 3

STEP 4

STEP 5

**TIPS**

Boxing is boring without opponents!
Think up other boxers to mash-up.
An eight-legged octo-boxer could be
a challenge. Or what about a mule
that boxes with its back legs?

FINAL!

# OCTO-SPY

Octopuses have no bones, and can fit into super small spaces. That means this octo-spy could be hiding anywhere! High seas treason is a thing of the past when the agent can squeeze its way into any room.

STEP 1

STEP 2

STEP 3

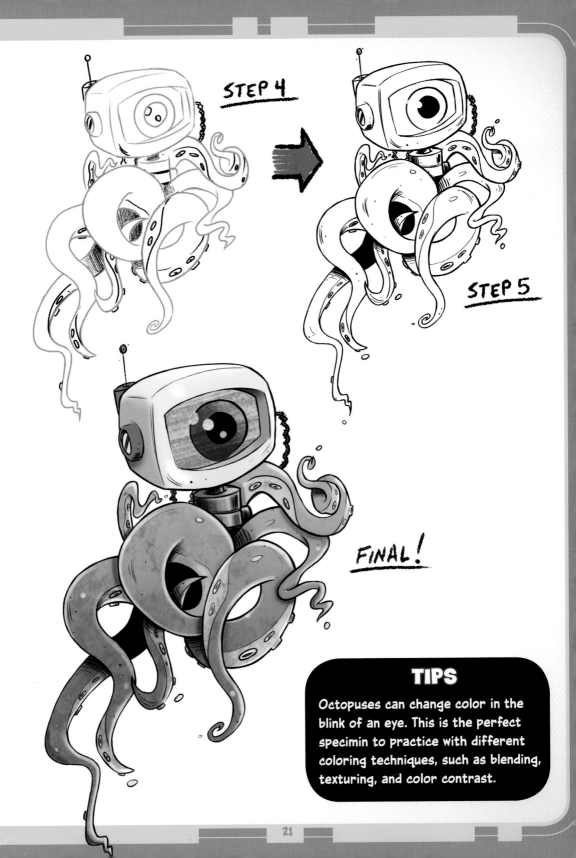

STEP 4

STEP 5

FINAL!

## TIPS

Octopuses can change color in the blink of an eye. This is the perfect specimin to practice with different coloring techniques, such as blending, texturing, and color contrast.

# READ OWL ABOUT IT

Mind your Ps and Qs with this wise old O-W-L. Professor Spectacles will have you R-E-A-D-I-N-G and S-P-E-L-L-I-N-G like a champ.

STEP 1

STEP 2

STEP 3

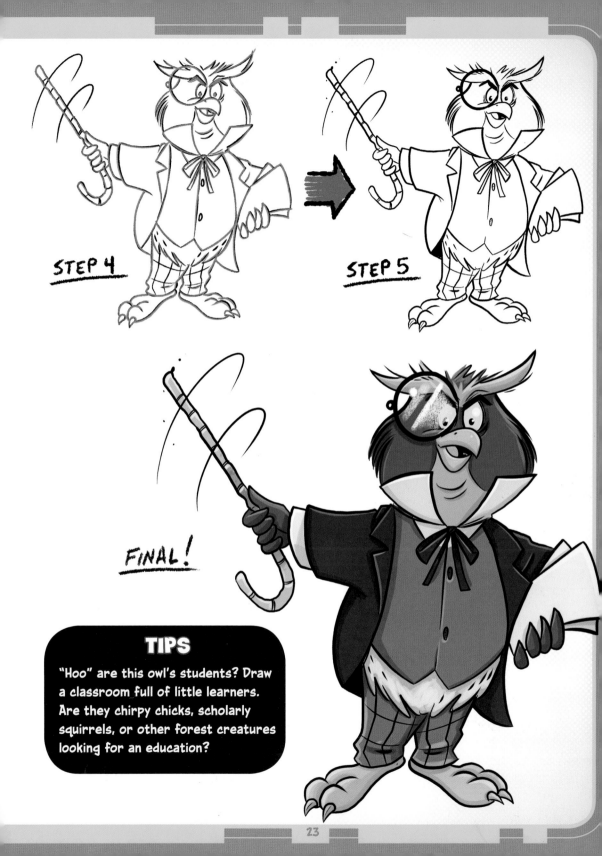

**STEP 4**

**STEP 5**

**FINAL!**

## TIPS

"Hoo" are this owl's students? Draw a classroom full of little learners. Are they chirpy chicks, scholarly squirrels, or other forest creatures looking for an education?

# ENDANGEROUS

Good luck taking down a rhino covered in armor!
Poachers are hunters who capture or kill animals illegally.
This rhino is angry and ready to poach the poachers back.

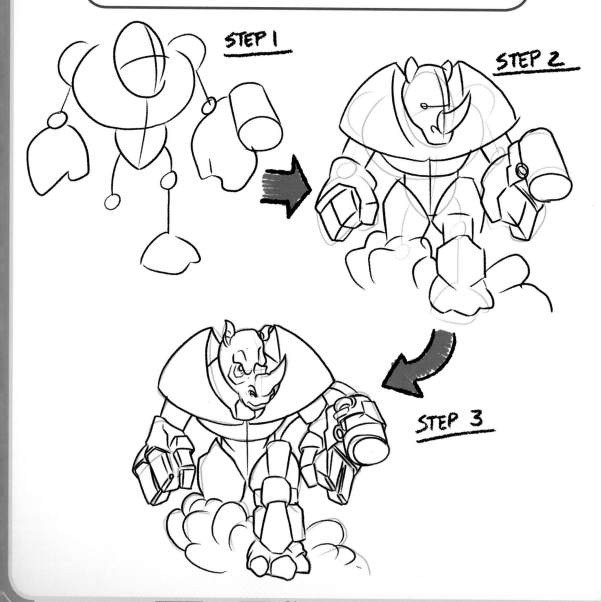

STEP 1

STEP 2

STEP 3

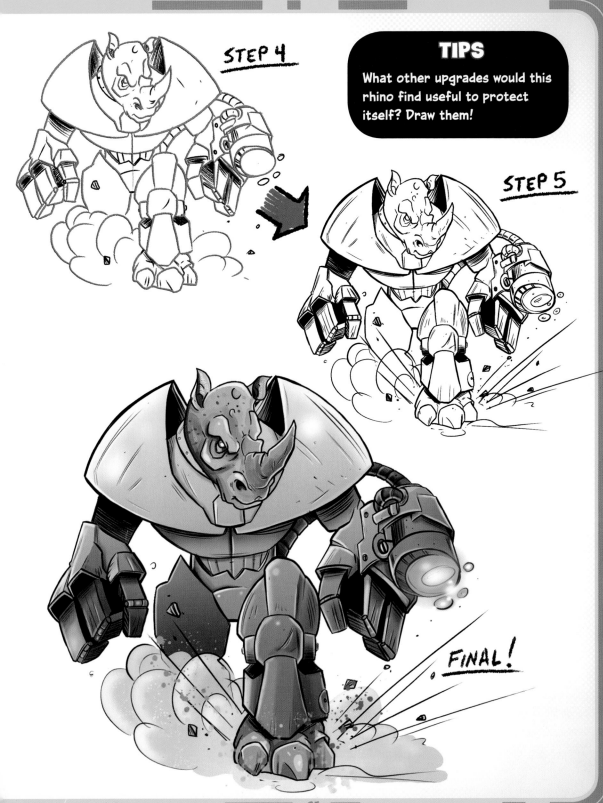

STEP 4

**TIPS**

What other upgrades would this rhino find useful to protect itself? Draw them!

STEP 5

FINAL!

# MEGALO-DIVE

Go 30,000 leagues under the sea in this fearsome underwater vessel. Not even the Mariana Trench at the bottom of the ocean is beyond your reach in a shark-marine.

**STEP 1**

**STEP 2**

**STEP 3**

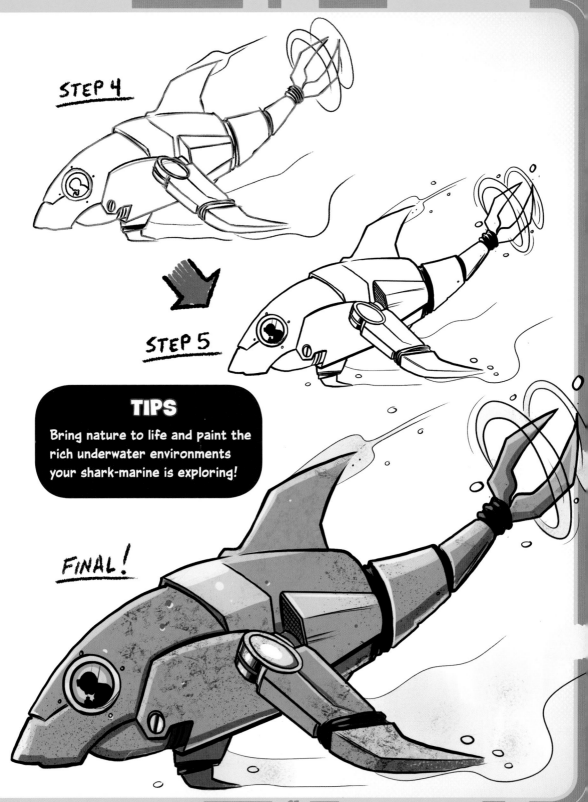

STEP 4

STEP 5

**TIPS**

Bring nature to life and paint the rich underwater environments your shark-marine is exploring!

FINAL!

# ROYAL SQUIRREL GUARD

No one gets past this squirrel sentry. Whether he's guarding the royal family or just their supply of winter seeds and nuts, he's always alert.

STEP 1

STEP 2

STEP 3

**STEP 4**

**STEP 5**

**FINAL!**

# TORTOISE TANK

At a top speed of 6.2 miles (10 kilometers) per month, this tortoise won't get to the battlefront right away, especially while fully armed. But he'll be there at the very end — the very, very end.

**STEP 1**

**STEP 2**

**STEP 3**

STEP 4

**TIPS**

Give your tortoise a boost! Add a jet pack or propellers for more speed. What would it look like with a tank's track wheels?

STEP 5

FINAL!

# READ MORE

Bird, Benjamin. *Animal Doodles with Scooby-Doo!* North Mankato, Minn.: Capstone Press, 2017.

Gowen, Fiona. *How to Draw Amazing Birds: From Songbirds to Birds of Prey.* Hauppauge, N.Y.: Barrons Educational Series, Inc., 2017.

Lajiness, Katie. *Dinosaurs.* Minneapolis: ABDO Pub., 2017.

# INTERNET SITES

Use FactHound to find Internet sites related to this book.

Visit *www.facthound.com*

Just type in 9781515769361 and go.